Crochet
TECHNIQUES & TIPS

Publications International, Ltd.

Consultant: Heidi Beazley

Written by Beth Taylor

Photo styling by Amy Stark

Photography by Christopher Hiltz

Additional photography © Shutterstock.com, Thinkstock, and Getty Images

Louis Weber, CEO
Publications International, Ltd.
8140 Lehigh Avenue
Morton Grove, Illinois 60053

www.pilbooks.com

ISBN: 978-1-4508-8256-9

Manufactured in China.

8 7 6 5 4 3 2 1

Table of Contents

Supplies

HOOKS, YARN & MATERIALS

What You'll Need

Crochet Hooks

Crochet hooks can be made from aluminum, plastic, wood, or bamboo. They are available in a wide range of sizes and are used with an assortment of yarns. Steel hooks are the smallest and are often used with fine thread in delicate crochet work, such as lace and doilies. Most patterns and yarn labels recommend a hook size. Select a crochet hook that feels comfortable to you and works well with your project and yarn.

Common Hook Sizes

US	B-1	C-2	D-3	E-4	F-5	G-6	7	H-8	I-9	J-10	K-10.5	L-11	M-13	N-15	P	Q	S
MM	2.25	2.75	3.25	3.5	3.75	4	4.5	5	5.5	6	6.5	8	9	10	15	16	19

Needles

Tapestry or yarn needles have a blunt tip and an eye large enough to accommodate thick yarns. These special needles can be used to weave in yarn ends or sew crocheted pieces together.

Stitch Markers

As their name suggests, stitch markers are designed to mark your stitches. They can be used to mark a certain number of stitches, the beginning of a round, or where to make a particular stitch. Stitch markers must have openings so that they can be easily removed. You can purchase stitch markers, or improvise with pins, earrings, or safety pins.

Pins

Use long, rustproof pins for blocking and pinning seams together. Pins can also serve as stitch markers. Opt for pins with large, colorful heads that won't get lost in your crochet work.

Measurement Tools

Measuring tape is a must-have tool when taking body measurements before making garments. Measuring tape and rulers can be used to measure gauge.

All About Yarn

Yarn for Beginners

Before starting any new crochet project, you must select your yarn. For beginners learning the basic stitches, select a simple cotton yarn that is light colored, smooth, and sturdy. It's harder to see your stitches with dark colored yarn. Avoid fuzzy and loosely woven yarns that fray easily.

Yarn Fibers

Natural fibers

Cotton, linen, and hemp yarns are made from plant fibers. They are lightweight, breathable, and machine washable. Mercerized cotton has undergone a chemical process that results in stronger, shinier yarn.

Yarns made from animal fibers include wool, silk, cashmere, mohair, alpaca, and angora. These animal fibers are much warmer than plant fibers. Both natural fibers offer a bit of stretch.

Synthetic fibers

Yarns made from synthetic fibers include nylon, rayon, acrylic, and polyester. Synthetic yarns are usually less expensive than natural fibers, but are less breathable and pill more easily.

Novelty and specialty yarns

Novelty and specialty yarns can be tricky to work with, but create a distinctive look. They include bouclé, ladder, eyelash, and chenille. While great for trims and accessories, novelty yarn is not best for beginners.

Selecting Your Yarn

Each package of store-bought yarn has a label listing the yarn's length, fiber content, and weight. Yarn weight refers to the thickness of a yarn. It ranges from thinnest embroidery thread to the bulkiest yarn. Yarn labels also recommend hook size—just look for the crochet hook symbol to find the U.S. and metric hook size.

Yarn Weight Guidelines

You can use these guidelines to help you select the appropriate hook size and yarn.

Yarn types: Fingering, lace, and 10-count crochet thread
Recommended hook sizes (metric): 1.5–2.25 mm
Recommended hook sizes (U.S.): Steel 6 to B-1
Crochet gauge range: 32–42 double crochet stitches to 4 in.

Yarn types: Sock, fingering, and baby
Recommended hook sizes (metric): 2.25–3.5 mm
Recommended hook sizes (U.S.): B-1 to E-4
Crochet gauge range: 21–32 single crochet stitches to 4 in.

Yarn types: Sport and baby
Recommended hook sizes (metric): 3.5–4.5 mm
Recommended hook sizes (U.S.): E-4 to 7
Crochet gauge range: 16–20 single crochet stitches to 4 in.

Yarn types: Double knitting and light worsted
Recommended hook sizes (metric): 4.5–5.5 mm
Recommended hook sizes (U.S.): 7 to I-9
Crochet gauge range: 12–17 single crochet stitches to 4 in.

Yarn types: Afghan, aran, and worsted
Recommended hook sizes (metric): 5.5–6.5 mm
Recommended hook sizes (U.S.): I-9 to K-10.5
Crochet gauge range: 11–14 single crochet stitches to 4 in.

Yarn types: Chunky, craft, and rug
Recommended hook sizes (metric): 6.5–9 mm
Recommended hook sizes (U.S.): K-10.5 to M-13
Crochet gauge range: 8–11 single crochet stitches to 4 in.

Yarn types: Bulky, super chunky, and roving
Recommended hook sizes (metric): 9 mm and larger
Recommended hook sizes (U.S.): M-13 and larger
Crochet gauge range: 5–9 single crochet stitches to 4 in.

Source: Craft Yarn Council's www.YarnStandards.com

Holding the Hook

Pencil Hold

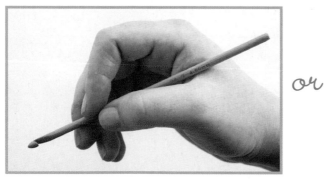

or

Knife Hold

Tip: The instructions and photographs in this book are intended for right-handed crocheters. If you are a lefty, try holding up a mirror to the edge of a photograph to see the left-handed version.

Holding the Yarn

1

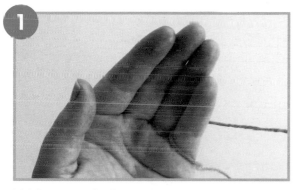

With your palm facing up, weave the working yarn (the yarn coming from the ball) between your pinky and ring fingers. Wrap the yarn clockwise around your pinky.

2

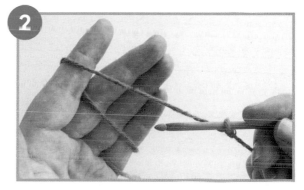

Take the yarn across your ring and middle fingers. Then wrap the yarn under and around your index finger.

3

Hold the yarn under the slip knot with your left thumb and middle finger.

Tip: There are many ways to hold your yarn. Experiment with different methods until you find what is most comfortable for you.

Making a Slip Knot

The first step in any crochet project is a slip knot.
The slip knot is what attaches the yarn to your hook.

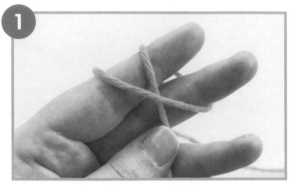

Wrap the yarn around your index and middle fingers on your yarn hand to create an X.

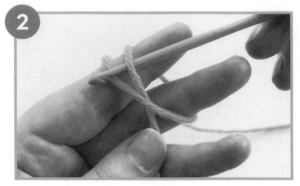

From the top, insert your hook under the first loop to grab the second loop.

Draw the second loop you just grabbed under and up through the first loop.

Slide your fingers out. Pull your hook up while gently pulling both ends of the yarn down.

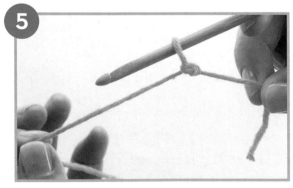

Pull the ends of the yarn to tighten the slip knot close to your hook.

With a finished slip knot around your hook, you are ready to start crocheting.

Chain Stitch (ch)

Crochet often begins with a series of chain stitches used to make up the first row. This is called the foundation chain and is the basic start to most crochet projects.

1

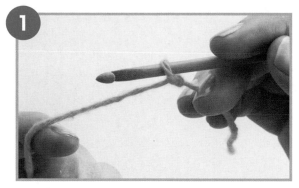

Start with a slip knot on your hook. Hold the yarn tail for tension.

2

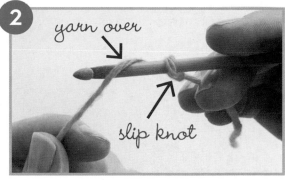

yarn over

slip knot

Bring the working yarn (the yarn coming from the ball) over your hook from back to front. This is called yarn over (yo).

3

Draw this section of yarn back through the slip knot. You will have 1 new loop on your hook when your first chain stitch is complete.

4

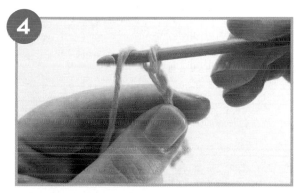

Yarn over again.

5

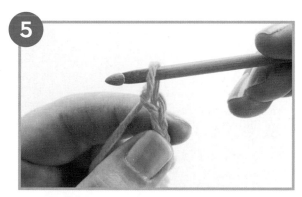

Draw this section of yarn through the loop on your hook. You will have 1 new loop on your hook each time you complete a chain stitch.

6

Repeat steps 2–3 until your foundation chain has the required number of chain stitches.

Tension

Tension keeps your stitches neat and consistent. Make sure the chains in your foundation chain are even and loose enough to allow your hook back into those chains for the next row.

Too loose

Too tight

Just right

Slip Stitch (sl st)

The slip stitch is one of the most basic crochet stitches and is often used for joining.

Start with a foundation chain on your hook. Insert your hook from front to back into the second chain from your hook. There are 2 loops on your hook.

Yarn over, bringing the working yarn over your hook from back to front.

Draw the yarn through both loops on your hook. You will have 1 new loop on your hook when your first slip stitch is complete.

Counting Chains

Crochet patterns usually begin by telling you the number of chains needed for the foundation chain.

Identifying the Front and Back

The front of the foundation chain looks like a braid with a series of Vs. The back side of the foundation chain has a vertical ridge of bumps running down the middle from your hook to the end of the chain. Count chains from the front side.

Front **Back**

Counting

Begin counting from the top of the foundation chain. (You can also count from the bottom up.) Do not count the loop on your hook or the slip knot on the bottom. Count only completed, V-shaped chain stitches. This example has 13 completed chain stitches.

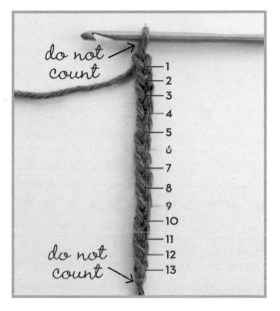

do not count

1
2
3
4
5
6
7
8
9
10
11
12
13

do not count

Tip: When creating a long foundation chain, it is helpful to use stitch markers every 10 or 20 stitches to make counting easier.

Turning Chains (tch)

Stitch	Number of Turning Chains
Single crochet	1
Half double crochet	2
Double crochet	3
Treble crochet	4

Each of the 4 basic crochet stitches requires a specific number of turning chains at the beginning or end of a row. The number of extra stitches needed for the turning chain is added to the number needed for the foundation chain.

Single Crochet (sc)

How to single crochet:

To begin a row of single crochet, first stitch a foundation chain to the desired length. Add 1 extra chain stitch for the turning chain.

insert your hook into this stitch

Insert your hook from front to back into the second chain stitch from your hook. There will now be 2 loops on your hook.

Yarn over. Draw this yarn through the first loop on your hook. There will be 2 loops on your hook.

3

Yarn over again and draw this yarn through both loops on your hook. You will have 1 loop remaining on your hook when your first single crochet is complete.

4

insert your hook into this stitch

Insert your hook into the next chain stitch. Repeat steps 2–3 to complete another single crochet stitch.

5

Repeat step 4, working a single crochet stitch into each chain. At the end of the row, make 1 chain stitch for the turning chain.

6

insert your hook into this stitch

Turn your work so that the opposite side faces you. Insert your hook into the first single crochet stitch of the previous row and repeat steps 2–3. (Skip the turning chain.)

7

Insert your hook into the next stitch and repeat steps 2–3, working a single crochet stitch into each single crochet of the previous row.

8

Repeat step 7 to continue the pattern. At the end of all rows, chain 1 for the turning chain, turn, and insert your hook into the next stitch.

Half Double Crochet (hdc)

How to half double crochet:

To begin a row of half double crochet, first stitch a foundation chain to the desired length. Add 2 extra chain stitches for the turning chain.

1 insert your hook into this stitch

Yarn over. With this yarn over, insert your hook into the third chain stitch from your hook. There will be 3 loops on your hook.

2

Yarn over again. Draw the yarn through the first loop only. There will still be 3 loops on your hook.

3 Yarn over and draw the yarn through all 3 loops on your hook.

4 You will have 1 loop on your hook when your first half double crochet stitch is complete.

5 *insert your hook into this stitch*

Yarn over. With this yarn over, insert your hook into the next chain stitch. There will be 3 loops on your hook. Repeat steps 2–4 to complete another half double crochet stitch.

6 Repeat step 5, working a half double crochet stitch into each chain stitch. At the end of the row, chain 2 for the turning chain.

7 *insert your hook into this stitch*

Turn your work so that the opposite side faces you. Yarn over and insert your hook into the second stitch. (The turning chain counts as the first half double crochet stitch in this row.) Repeat steps 2–4 to complete the stitch.

8 Repeat step 5 to continue making half double crochet stitches into each stitch of the previous row. At the end of this and all subsequent rows, chain 2 for the turning chain and turn.

Double Crochet (dc)

How to double crochet:

To begin a row of double crochet, first stitch a foundation chain to the desired length. Add 3 extra chain stitches for the turning chain.

insert your hook into this stitch

Yarn over. With this yarn over, insert your hook into the fourth chain stitch from your hook. There will be 3 loops on your hook.

Yarn over. Draw the yarn through the first loop on your hook. There will be 3 loops on your hook.

Yarn over. Draw the yarn through the first 2 loops on your hook only. There will now be 2 loops on your hook.

Yarn over again. Draw the yarn through the remaining 2 loops on your hook. You will have 1 loop on your hook when your first double crochet stitch is complete.

Yarn over. Insert your hook into the next chain stitch. Repeat steps 2–4 to complete another double crochet stitch.

insert your hook into this stitch

Repeat step 5, working a double crochet stitch into each chain stitch. At the end of the row, chain 3 for the turning chain. Turn your work so that the opposite side faces you.

insert your hook into this stitch

Yarn over and insert your hook into the second stitch. (The turning chain counts as the first double crochet stitch in this row.) Repeat steps 2–4 to complete the stitch.

Repeat step 5 to continue making double crochet stitches into each stitch of the previous row. At the end of this and all subsequent rows, chain 3 for the turning chain and turn.

Treble Crochet (tr)

How to treble crochet:

To begin a row of treble crochet, first stitch a foundation chain to the desired length. Add 4 extra chain stitches for the turning chain.

insert your hook into this stitch →

Yarn over twice. Insert your hook into the fifth chain stitch from your hook. There will be 4 loops on your hook.

Yarn over once. Draw the yarn through the first loop on your hook. There will be 4 loops on your hook.

3

Yarn over once. Draw the yarn through the first 2 loops on your hook. There will be 3 loops on your hook.

4

Yarn over once. Draw the yarn through the first 2 loops on your hook again. There will be 2 loops on your hook.

5

Yarn over. Draw the yarn through the remaining 2 loops on your hook. You will have 1 loop on your hook when your first treble crochet stitch is complete.

6

insert your hook into this stitch

Yarn over twice and insert your hook into the next chain stitch. Repeat steps 2–5 to complete another treble crochet stitch.

7

insert your hook into this stitch

Repeat step 6, working a treble crochet stitch into each chain. At the end of the row, chain 4 for the turning chain. Turn your work so that the opposite side faces you. Yarn over twice and insert your hook into the second stitch. Repeat steps 2–5 to complete the treble crochet stitch.

8

Repeat step 6 to continue making treble crochet stitches into each stitch of the previous row. At the end of this and all subsequent rows, chain 4 for the turning chain, yarn over twice, and insert your hook into the second stitch.

Decreasing Stitches (dec)

To decrease within a row, combine multiple stitches together.

Single Crochet Decrease

insert your hook into this stitch

Insert your hook into the next stitch as you would to start a single crochet.

Yarn over and draw the yarn through the stitch. There are now 2 loops on your hook.

Insert your hook into the next stitch. Yarn over and draw the yarn through the stitch. There are 3 loops on your hook.

Yarn over and draw the yarn through all 3 loops on your hook. You will have 1 loop on your hook when your first decrease is complete.

Double Crochet Decrease

Yarn over and insert your hook into the next stitch. Yarn over and draw the yarn through the stitch. Yarn over and draw the yarn through the first 2 loops. You will have 2 loops on your hook.

Yarn over and insert your hook into the next stitch. Yarn over and draw the yarn through the stitch. Yarn over and draw the yarn through the first 2 loops. You will have 3 loops on your hook.

3

Yarn over and draw the yarn through all 3 loops on your hook. You will have 1 loop on your hook when your first decrease is complete.

Increasing Stitches (inc)

To increase within a row, work multiple stitches into the same stitch.

Single Crochet Increase

1

Insert your hook back into the same stitch you did your last single crochet in. Work another single crochet into that same stitch.

2

You will have 1 loop on your hook when your first single crochet increase is complete.

Double Crochet Increase

1

Insert your hook back into the same stitch in the previous row. Work another double crochet into that same stitch.

2

You will have 1 loop on your hook when your first double crochet increase is complete.

Front & Back Loops (FL & BL)

Working into the front or back loop only will create a unique texture and line.
These examples use half double crochet, but you can use these techniques with other stitches.

Tip: When your crochet work is in front of you, the front loop is the loop closer to you, while the back loop is farther from you.

front loop   back loop

Front Loops

1

To work a half double crochet stitch into the front loop, yarn over and insert your hook into only the front loop facing you. Complete the stitch as usual.

2

Continue working half double crochet stitches into only the front loops of the stitches in the previous row until you reach the end of the row. This creates a line.

Back Loops

1

To work a half double crochet stitch into the back loop, yarn over and insert your hook into only the back loop facing away from you. Complete the stitch as usual.

2

Continue working half double crochet stitches into only the back loops of the stitches in the previous row until you reach the end of the row. This creates another line.

Working into Spaces

Some patterns will ask you to work into a space rather than a stitch of a previous row or round. This technique is demonstrated below using double crochet.

Start at the position where you want to work into a space. Yarn over.

Insert your hook from front to back into the space (instead of the stitch). Yarn over and pull the yarn through the space.

Finish your double crochet as usual. You will have 1 loop on your hook when your first double crochet stitch into the space is complete.

Here is the row finished with double crochet stitches worked into the spaces.

Tip: Working into spaces is often called for when starting a round and in many floral motifs. In the example to the right, multiple stitches have been made into the spaces.

Working in Rounds

To begin working in rounds, you have to first start with a center ring.
There are 2 different methods for starting a round, with a chain stitch ring or a magic circle.

Chain Stitch Ring

The chain stitch ring is made up of chain stitches that are joined together to form a ring. This method leaves a small opening in the center of your round.

Tip: Patterns will tell you how many chains to start with and what stitches to use. This example uses single crochet.

Chain 5 for a foundation chain. Insert your hook back into the first chain you made.

Work a slip stitch into that chain to form a ring.

Insert your hook into the center of the ring. Work a single crochet stitch into the ring.

Continue working single crochet stitches into the ring until you have made the required number of stitches. (For this example, 6 single crochet stitches.)

Work a slip stitch into the first single crochet you made to close up the ring.

You are now ready to start a round. (See page 29.)

Magic Circle

The magic circle forms a ring with your yarn that your first round of stitches are attached to. The ends are pulled to leave no opening in the center. That's the magic!

Tip: A chain stitch ring can replace a magic circle in a pattern.

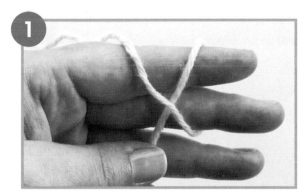

Loop the yarn around your fingers as shown to form an X.

Take your hook under the bottom strand of the X. Use your hook to draw the other strand under the bottom strand. It will form a loose loop on your hook.

Remove the circle of yarn from your fingers. Yarn over. Draw the yarn through the loop on your hook. (This does not count as your first single crochet stitch.)

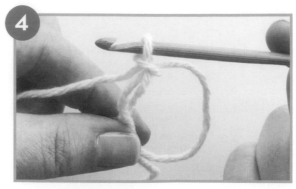

You should now have a circle with the tail and the working yarn on the left side.

Insert your hook into the center of the circle. You are going to work a single crochet into that space. Yarn over and draw the yarn through the circle and tail. You will have 2 loops on your hook.

Yarn over again and draw the yarn through the remaining 2 loops on your hook. You will have 1 loop on your hook when your first single crochet stitch into the circle is complete.

Continue working the required number of single crochet stitches into the circle, making sure you are always working around the circle and the tail. If you run out of tail, pull it slightly. This closes the circle a little, but allows you to have a longer tail to work around.

When you have worked 6 single crochet stitches into the circle, pull the tail tightly to close the circle.

Insert your hook into the first single crochet stitch you made and make a slip stitch to close the circle.

With your slip stitch complete, you are now ready to start a round.

Starting a Round

To start a round, first begin by using either the chain stitch ring or magic circle method. This example used the magic circle method.

Round 1:

insert your hook under these 2 loops

Chain 1. Insert your hook under the top 2 loops of the first stitch and work a single crochet into that stitch.

Work 2 single crochets into each of the remaining stitches. (You will have 12 stitches.) Insert your hook back into the first stitch and make a slip stitch to close the round.

Rounds 2-6:

Each round increases by 6 stitches. The increases are evenly spaced in order to keep the circular shape. Close each round with a slip stitch back into the first stitch and then chain 1.

Round 2: Single crochet an increase in every other stitch for a total of 18 stitches.
Round 3: Single crochet an increase in every third stitch for a total of 24 stitches.
Round 4: Single crochet an increase in every fourth stitch for a total of 30 stitches.
Round 5: Single crochet an increase in every fifth stitch for a total of 36 stitches.
Round 6: Single crochet an increase in every sixth stitch for a total of 42 stitches.

For additional rounds, continue to evenly increase your rounds by 6 until your desired circumference.

Joining in New Yarn

At the End of a Row

To join in new yarn at the end of a row, work the last stitch with the old yarn until the final yarn over of the stitch. Yarn over with the new yarn.

Draw the new yarn through both loops on your hook. There is 1 loop on your hook. Continue stitching with the new yarn as usual.

In the Middle of a Row

To join in new yarn in the middle of a row, work the last stitch with the old yarn until the final yarn over of the stitch. Yarn over with the new yarn.

Draw the new yarn through both loops on your hook. There is 1 loop on your hook. Continue stitching with the new yarn as usual until you reach the end of the row.

Tip: Rather than leaving the tail of the old yarn in the middle of the row, you can work over the old yarn until you reach the end of the row. You can then weave in all yarn tails at the edges later.

Fastening Off

1

After completing your last stitch, cut the excess yarn, leaving several inches to weave the tail in later. Yarn over and draw the yarn tail through the loop on your hook.

2

Pull the yarn tail to tighten.

Weaving in the Tail

1

Thread one of your yarn tails into a blunt-tipped needle. Insert the needle into the first stitch and draw the yarn through.

2

Continue weaving the needle under and over the stitches around the edge.

3

Cut the yarn close to the final stitch when you're done weaving in the tail.

Stitches

PUTTING THE BASICS TOGETHER

Double Herringbone (HBdc)

The double herringbone stitch is basically a modified double crochet stitch. To make a double herringbone stitch, start with a foundation chain.

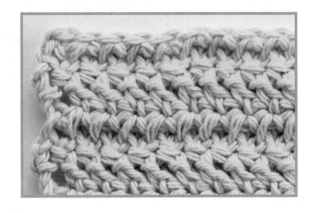

1 Yarn over and insert your hook into the third chain from your hook. There are 3 loops on your hook.

2 Yarn over and draw the yarn through the first 2 loops on your hook. There are 2 loops on your hook.

3 Yarn over and draw the yarn through the first loop on your hook. There are still 2 loops on your hook.

4 Yarn over and draw the yarn through both loops on your hook. You will have 1 loop on your hook when your first HBdc stitch is complete.

5

Continue to the end of the row. Chain 3 for the turning chain. Turn your work so the opposite side faces you. Skip the 3 turning chains and the first stitch. Yarn over and insert your hook into the next stitch.

Repeat steps 2–5 to continue the pattern.

Crossed Stitches

Crossed stitches cross back over the front of previous stitches to form a unique X pattern. Double and treble crochet are the most common stitches used to cross.

To make crossed stitches using double crochet, start with a foundation chain that has a multiple of 2 chains.

Row 1:

In the fifth chain from your hook, work 1 double crochet. There is 1 loop on your hook.

Crossing over the front of the double crochet you just made, work 1 double crochet into the last skipped chain.

You will have 1 loop on your hook when your first pair of crossed stitches is complete.

Chain 1. Skip 1 chain and work 1 double crochet into the next chain after that.

5

Crossing over the front of the double crochet you just made, work 1 double crochet into the last skipped chain.

6

Repeat steps 4–5 across the row. At the end of the row, work 1 double crochet into the last chain.

7

Chain 3 for the turning chain and turn your work so that the opposite side faces you.

Tip: **How to make crossed treble stitches:**

1. Start with an odd number foundation chain.

2. In the sixth chain from your hook, work 1 treble crochet stitch.

3. Follow steps 2–6, replacing double crochet with treble crochet stitches.

4. Chain 4 for the turning chain and turn.

Row 2:

1. Skip the first 2 stitches and work 1 double crochet into the next double crochet stitch.

2. Crossing over the front of the double crochet you just made, work 1 double crochet into the last skipped stitch.

3. Chain 1. Skip the next double crochet stitch and work 1 double crochet into the last skipped stitch.

4. Repeat step 3 until the last stitch of the row. Work 1 double crochet into the last stitch.

5. Chain 3 and turn.

Repeat row 2 to continue the pattern.

Popcorns (pc)

The popcorn stitch works several stitches into the same space, resulting in a "puffed" pattern and texture.

To make a popcorn using single and double crochet, start with a foundation chain that has a multiple of 3 chain stitches.

Row 1:

Work 1 single crochet into the second chain from your hook.

Finish the row with single crochet stitches. Chain 1 for the turning chain.

Row 2:

Turn your work so the opposite side faces you. Work a single crochet into each of the next 2 stitches.

In the next stitch, work 5 double crochets into the same stitch. Drop the loop you created by removing your hook.

Insert your hook under the top 2 loops of the first double crochet of the group.

Grab the dropped loop with your hook and draw the yarn through the stitch. Add a chain stitch to complete your first popcorn stitch. You will have 1 loop on your hook.

Work 1 single crochet into each of the next 3 stitches.

Continue to the end of the row, alternating between the popcorn stitch and the single crochet stitches. At the end of row, chain 1 for the turning chain.

Row 3:

Turn your work so the opposite side faces you. Work 1 single crochet stitch into each stitch across the row.

Tip: For rows of staggered popcorn stitches like in our example swatch, reduce the number of single crochet stitches at the beginning of every other popcorn row. Then complete the popcorn rows as usual.

Repeat rows 2–3 to continue the pattern.

V-Stitch

The V-stitch makes a series of interlocking Vs. This stitch works up quickly and is great for making afghans.

To make V-stitches using double crochet, start with a foundation chain that has a multiple of 3 chains, plus 7.

Row 1:

Work 1 double crochet into the fourth chain from your hook. Chain 1.

Skip 1 chain stitch and work 1 double crochet into the next chain. Chain 1.

Work 1 double crochet into the very same chain. You will have 1 loop on your hook when your first V-stitch is complete.

Skip 2 chains and work 1 double crochet into the next chain. Chain 1. Work 1 double crochet into the very same stitch.

Repeat step 4 across the row until you have 4 chains left. Chain 1.

Skip 2 chains. Work 1 double crochet into each of the last 2 chains to end the row.

At the end of the row, chain 3 for the turning chain. Turn your work so the opposite side faces you.

Tip: A chain 1 space is the space created by the chain 1 between the 2 double crochet stitches. It looks like the center of a V.

this is a chain 1 space →

Row 2:

The turning chain counts as the first double crochet in this row. Work 1 double crochet into the next stitch and chain 1.

Work 1 V-stitch into each chain 1 space (center of each V) across the row until you have 1 chain space and 2 double crochet stitches left.

3 When you have 1 chain space and 2 double crochet stitches left, chain 1 and skip the chain 1 space. Work 1 double crochet into each of the last 2 double crochet stitches to end the row. Chain 3 for the turning chain and turn.

Repeat row 2 to continue the pattern.

Chevrons

A chevron is a classic stitch pattern that is great for baby blankets. Try alternating colors to accentuate the pattern. This example works 3 double crochets into 1 stitch to create the points.

To make chevrons using double crochet, start with a foundation chain that has a multiple of 10 chains, plus 1.

Row 1:

1 In the third chain from your hook, work 1 double crochet. (The skipped chains count as 1 double crochet.)

2 Work 1 double crochet into each of the next 3 chains.

3 Over the next 3 chain stitches, work 3 double crochet stitches together (dc3tog) to decrease.

4 Work 1 double crochet into each of the next 3 chains.

Tip: Depending on how many chain stitches you've done, subsequent rows will sometimes start at a peak and other times at a valley. Just make sure your increases (peaks) and decreases (valleys) in each row line up.

5

Work 3 double crochets into the next chain.

6

Repeat steps 2–5 until you reach the last chain.

7

Work 2 double crochet stitches into the last chain of the row.

8

Chain 3 for the turning chain (counts as 1 double crochet in the next row) and turn your work so that the opposite side faces you.

Row 2:

1. Work 1 double crochet into the first stitch of the row.

2. Work 1 double crochet into each of the next 3 double crochet stitches.

3. Over the next 3 stitches, work 3 double crochet stitches together (dc3tog) to decrease.

4. Work 1 double crochet into each of the next 3 double crochet stitches.

5. Work 3 double crochet stitches into the next stitch.

6. Repeat steps 2–5 across the second row, ending with 2 double crochet stitches worked into the top of the turning chain. Chain 3 for the turning chain and turn your work.

Repeat row 2 to continue the pattern.

Shell Stitch

Shells are created by working several stitches into the same stitch or space. They are also referred to as a fan stitch.

To make shell stitches using single and double crochet, start with a foundation chain that has a multiple of 4 chains, plus 1.

Row 1:

1 In the fifth chain from your hook, work 4 double crochet stitches.

2 Skip the next 3 chains and work 4 double crochet stitches into the next chain.

3 Repeat step 2 across the row until there are 4 chains left. Skip 3 chains and work 2 double crochet stitches into the last chain. Chain 1 for the turning chain and turn your work so that the opposite side faces you.

Row 2:

1 Work 1 single crochet into each of the double crochet stitches from the previous row. Chain 3 for the turning chain and turn your work so that the opposite side faces you.

Row 3:

1. Work 1 double crochet into the first stitch. Skip 3 stitches.

2. Work 4 double crochets into the next single crochet stitch. Skip the next 3 single crochet stitches.

3. Repeat step 2 across the row until there are 2 stitches left.

4. Skip the next single crochet stitch and work 1 double crochet into the last stitch.

5. Chain 1 for the turning chain and turn your work so that the opposite side faces you.

Row 4:

1. Work 1 single crochet into the next double crochet.

2. Continue working 1 single crochet into each double crochet stitch across the row.

3. Work 1 single crochet stitch into the top of the turning chain from the previous row.

4. Chain 3 for the turning chain and turn your work so that the opposite side faces you.

Row 5.

1. Skip the first 2 single crochet stitches.

2. Work 4 double crochet stitches into the next single crochet.

3. Skip the next 3 single crochets.

4. Repeat steps 2–3 across the row until there are 2 stitches left.

5. Skip the next stitch and work 1 double crochet stitch into the last stitch of the previous row.

6. Chain 1 for the turning chain and turn your work so that the opposite side faces you.

Repeat rows 4–5 to continue the pattern.

Bobbles (bo)

Bobbles work multiple stitches together into 1 stitch or space. They work best with taller stitches like double and treble crochet.

To make bobbles using single and double crochet, start with a foundation chain that has any odd number of chains.

Row 1:

1 In the second chain from your hook, work 1 single crochet stitch.

2 Chain 1. Skip 1 chain and work 1 single crochet stitch into the next chain. Repeat step 2 across the row.

3 At the end of the row, chain 3 for the turning chain and turn your work so that the opposite side faces you.

Row 2:

1 Skip the first stitch. The turning chain counts as the first double crochet in this row.

Row 2 (continued):

2

In the next chain space, double crochet 5 together (dc5tog) following the tip instructions.

Tip: **How to double crochet 5 together:**

1. Yarn over. Insert your hook into the chain space.

2. Yarn over and draw the yarn through the space.

3. Yarn over and draw the yarn through the first 2 loops on your hook.

4. Repeat steps 1–3, inserting your hook into the same chain space, until you have 6 loops on your hook. Each time you repeat this process, you will add another loop to your hook.

3

On your final bobble, yarn over and draw the yarn through all 6 loops on your hook. You will have 1 loop on your hook when your 5 double crochets are complete.

4

Make 1 chain stitch to secure and complete the bobble.

5

Repeat steps 2–4 across the row, ending with 1 double crochet in the last single crochet of the row. Chain 1 for the turning chain and turn your work.

Row 3:

1. Work 1 single crochet into the first stitch.

2. Chain 1. Skip 1 chain and work 1 single crochet into the next stitch.

3. Repeat step 2 across the row.

Repeat rows 2–3 to continue the pattern.

Clusters (CL)

You make clusters by combining stitches together into the same stitch or space.

To make cluster stitches using single crochet, start with a foundation chain that has a multiple of 2 chains, plus 1.

$\mathcal{T}ip$: **How to single crochet 2 together using 2 chain spaces:**

1. Insert your hook into the chain space to be worked.

2. Yarn over and draw the yarn through the space. You will have 2 loops on your hook.

3. Insert your hook into the next chain space.

4. Yarn over and draw the yarn through the space. There will be 3 loops on your hook.

5. Yarn over and draw the yarn through all 3 loops on your hook. There will be 1 loop left on your hook.

these are the chain spaces

Row 1:

In the second chain from your hook, work 1 single crochet stitch.

Chain 1. Skip 1 chain and work 1 single crochet into the next chain. Repeat step 2 across the row. Chain 1 for the turning chain.

Row 2:

1
Turn your work so that the opposite side faces you. Work 1 single crochet into the first stitch of the row. Chain 1.

2
Following the tip instructions, single crochet 2 together (sc2tog), working into the next 2 chain spaces. Chain 1 when you're finished.

3
work back into this chain space

Insert your hook back into the chain space you just worked in. Single crochet 2 together using this chain space and the next. Chain 1.

4
Repeat step 3 across the row, ending the row with 1 single crochet in the last stitch. Chain 1 for the turning chain and turn your work so that the opposite side faces you.

Row 3:

1. Work 1 single crochet into the first stitch.

2. Chain 1.

3. Skip 1 chain and work 1 single crochet into the next stitch.

4. Repeat steps 2–3 across the row.

Repeat rows 2–3 to continue the pattern.

Seed Stitch

Each seed stitch consists of 1 single crochet and 1 double crochet worked into the same chain or stitch.

To make seed stitches, start with a foundation chain that has any odd number of chains.

Row 1:

1 In the second chain from your hook, work 1 single crochet stitch.

2 Work 1 double crochet into the very same chain. You will have 1 loop on your hook when your first seed stitch is complete.

3 Skip 1 chain and insert your hook into the next chain.

4 Work 1 single crochet into that chain. Work 1 double crochet into the very same chain. Your second seed stitch is complete.

5

Repeat steps 3–4 across the row, stitching 1 single crochet and 1 double crochet into every other chain in the foundation. Chain 2 for the turning chain.

Row 2:

1

Turn your work so that the opposite side faces you. The turning chain counts as the first single crochet in row 2. Work 1 double crochet into that same single crochet stitch.

2

Continue across the row, working 1 single crochet stitch and 1 double crochet stitch into each double crochet in the previous row.

Repeat row 2 to continue the pattern.

Tip: This stitch pattern will have a scalloped or wavy edge instead of a straight edge. It is great for washcloths, dishcloths, and potholders!

Puffs

Puff stitches are similar to bobbles.

To make puffs using half double crochet, start with a foundation chain that has any odd number of chains.

Tip: **How to half double crochet 4 together:**

1. Yarn over and insert your hook into the chain space.

2. Yarn over and draw the loop through. You will have 3 loops on your hook.
It's important to keep your loops taller so it's easier to draw through them at the end.

3. Repeat steps 1–2 two more times until you have 7 loops on your hook.
(With every repeat, you add 2 more loops to your hook.)

4. Yarn over and draw through all 7 loops. There will be 1 loop left on your hook.

Row 1:

In the second chain from your hook, work 1 single crochet stitch.

Chain 1. Skip 1 chain and work 1 single crochet into the next chain. Repeat across the row.

3 At the end of the row, chain 2 for the turning chain and turn your work so the opposite side faces you.

Row 2:

1 Skip the first stitch. The turning chain counts as the first half double crochet in this row.

In the next chain space, work 4 half double crochet stitches together (hdc4tog) following the tip instructions, until you have 7 loops on your hook.

Yarn over and draw through all 7 loops on your hook. There will be 1 loop left when your 4 half double crochets are complete.

Chain 1 to secure and complete the puff.

Repeat steps 2–4 across the row, ending with 1 half double crochet in the last stitch of the previous row.

Chain 1 for the turning chain and turn your work so the opposite side faces you.

Row 3:

1. Work 1 single crochet into the first stitch.

2. Chain 1. Skip 1 chain and work 1 single crochet into the next stitch.

3. Repeat step 2 across the row.

Repeat rows 2–3 to continue the pattern.

Basket Weave

This basket weave uses alternating front-post double crochet (FPdc) and back-post double crochet (BPdc) stitches. Post stitches are sometimes called raised stitches.

Start with a foundation chain that has a multiple of 6 chains, plus 4.

About Front & Back Posts:

Instead of inserting your hook into a stitch or space, you insert it around the front or back of a post. The stitches are worked the same as usual. The only difference is where your hook is inserted.

posts

Front Posts:
Insert your hook under the post from the front side.

Back Posts:
Insert your hook under the post from the back side.

Row 1:

In the fourth chain from your hook, work 1 double crochet. Continue across the row, working 1 double crochet into each chain.

Chain 2 for the turning chain and turn your work so the opposite side faces you.

Row 2:

1

Work 1 double crochet around the second front post of the previous row (FPdc). To do this, yarn over (because you are doing a double crochet) and insert your hook under the second post. Finish your double crochet stitch as usual.

2

Work a FPdc stitch into the next 2 posts so there are a total of 3.

3

Work 1 double crochet around the next back post (BPdc). To do this, yarn over (because you are doing a double crochet) and insert your hook, from the back side, under the next post. Finish your double crochet stitch as usual.

4

Work a BPdc stitch into the next 2 posts so there are a total of 3.

5

Continue across the row, alternating 3 FPdc stitches with 3 BPdc stitches. Finish the row by working 1 double crochet into the top chain of the turning chain.

6

Chain 2 for the turning chain and turn your work so the opposite side faces you.

Row 3:

Repeat row 2, alternating 3 FPdc stitches with 3 BPdc stitches across the row. Work 1 double crochet into the top of the turning chain. Chain 2 and turn.

Row 4:

Work 1 BPdc stitch around the second post. Work 1 BPdc stitch around the next 2 posts for a total of 3 BPdc stitches.

Work 3 FPdc stitches around the next 3 posts. Continue across the row, alternating 3 BPdc stitches with 3 FPdc stitches.

3. Work 1 double crochet into the top of the last turning chain.

4. Chain 2 for the turning chain and turn your work so the opposite side faces you.

Row 5:

1. Repeat row 4, alternating 3 BPdc stitches with 3 FPdc stitches across the row. Work 1 double crochet into the top of the turning chain. Chain 2 and turn.

Repeat rows 2–5 to continue the pattern.

Finishing
EDGING & JOINING

Edging Techniques

There are many different edging techniques, which can be crocheted or sewn.
Each technique will give your piece a finished and unique look. Here are a few examples.

Shell Stitch Edge

The shells in this example are made from 5 double crochet stitches into the same single crochet stitch. Start with a row of single crochet around the edge of your piece.

1 Insert your hook into the single crochet stitch in the upper right-hand corner and secure the yarn with a slip stitch. Chain 3.

2 In the next stitch, work 2 double crochets.

3 Chain 1. Skip 1 stitch and work 1 single crochet into the next stitch.

4 Chain 1. Skip 1 stitch and work 5 double crochets into the next stitch. Your first 5-dc shell is complete.

5 Repeat steps 2–4 around your entire piece. End with 3 more double crochets in the same stitch you worked 2 double crochets into in step 2 to complete the 5-dc shell.

Picot Stitch Edge

Picot edges can either be made small or large. They can be worked into stitches or spaces and can be added to any row of stitches. Here picots are added to rows of single crochet.

Small picot

Large picot

Small Picot

Insert your hook anywhere along the edge and join your edging yarn with a slip stitch.

Chain 3. Insert your hook into the third chain from your hook. Yarn over and draw the yarn through both loops to complete 1 small picot.

Work 1 single crochet into each of the next 3 stitches.

 Alternate 1 small picot with 3 single crochet stitches around the edges.

Large Picot

1. Insert your hook anywhere along the edge and join your edging yarn with a slip stitch.

2. Chain 5. Insert your hook into the fifth chain from your hook. Yarn over and draw the yarn through both loops to complete 1 large picot.

3. Work 1 single crochet into each of the next 3 stitches.

4. Alternate 1 large picot with 3 single crochet stitches around the edges.

Crab Stitch Edge

Crab stitch is also called reverse single crochet.
Start with a row of single crochet along the edge.

1 Secure the new yarn with a slip stitch in the top left-hand corner.

2 Insert your hook into the same stitch you just worked into.

3 Yarn over and draw the yarn through the stitch (the first loop on your hook). There are 2 loops on your hook.

4 Yarn over again and draw the yarn through both loops on your hook. You will have 1 loop on your hook when your first crab stitch is complete.

5 Repeat steps 2–4 across the edge, working 1 crab stitch into each single crochet to the right.

Tip: To continue the edging around a corner, work multiple crab stitches into the same corner stitch.

Blanket Stitch Edge

The blanket stitch is sewn rather than crocheted. It lies flat and can help disguise uneven edges.

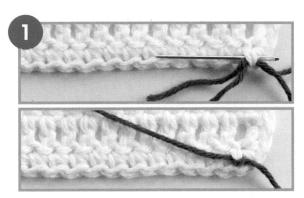

Thread the yarn through the large eye of a tapestry needle. With the wrong side facing up, secure the yarn to the bottom right-hand side of the crochet piece.

Flip the crochet piece so the right side is facing up. Draw the needle from back to front through the bottom left-hand side.

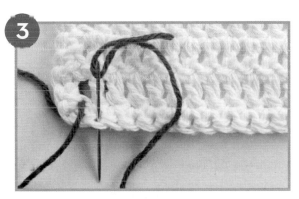

Insert the needle from front to back through the next small space on the edge.

Pull the needle through, going over the loop that was created. You have completed 1 blanket stitch.

5 Continue across the edge, working blanket stitches into the spaces between stitches.

Tip: To continue the edging around a corner, work multiple blanket stitches into the same corner space.

Joining Pieces Together

There are many techniques for joining pieces together, including both crochet and sewing methods. Some methods create a more bulky seam and will be more sturdy. Other methods are less bulky, but might be more delicate. Use the same yarn from your project to help disguise the seams. Using a different color yarn can add more detail to your project.

Single Crochet Join

To join crochet pieces together with single crochet, start by placing the pieces with right sides together and stitches or rows lined up.

Tip: The only difference between a regular row of single crochet stitches and a single crochet join is that you will be working each stitch in both pieces.

Front side   Back side

Insert your hook from front to back under the first pair of stitches on both pieces. Make a slip knot and attach it to the end of your hook.

Draw the slip knot through both pieces, letting the knot catch on the back. Yarn over and draw through the loop on your hook. Yarn over again and draw through both loops on your hook.

3 Insert your hook from front to back under the next pair of stitches and work a single crochet stitch.

4 Repeat step 3 across the seam, working 1 single crochet in each pair of stitches. When complete, fasten off and weave in yarn tails.

Slip Stitch Join

To join crochet pieces with slip stitch, start by placing the pieces with right sides together and stitches or rows lined up.

Tip: To make the slip stitch seam less bulky, try only working through 1 loop of each stitch.

Front side   Back side

Insert your hook from front to back under the first corresponding pair of stitches of both pieces on the right. Make a slip knot and attach it to the end of your hook.

Draw the slip knot through both pieces. The knot will catch on the back. Yarn over and draw the yarn through the loop on your hook.

Insert your hook from front to back under the next pair of corresponding stitches on the left. Yarn over and draw the yarn through both loops on your hook. You will have 1 loop on your hook when your first slip stitch is complete.

Repeat step 3 across the seam. When complete, fasten off and weave in yarn tails.

Ladder Stitch Join

The ladder stitch creates seams that are flat and nearly invisible (as long as you use the same color yarn).

To join 2 crochet pieces with ladder stitch, start by placing the pieces with right sides together and stitches or rows lined up.

Front side

Back side

1

On the top crochet piece, insert your threaded tapestry needle through the outside loop of the bottom left-hand stitch, and then through the same outside loop on the bottom piece.

2

Working in the opposite direction as your last stitch, bring your needle through only the outside loops of the next stitches above on both crochet pieces.

3

Repeat step 2 up the seam. Pull both yarn tails to tighten and weave in the tails.

Backstitch Join

The backstitch is a sewing method you can use to join crochet pieces together. It is extra strong, but bulky.

To join 2 crochet pieces with backstitch, start by placing the pieces with right sides together and stitches or rows lined up. Cut a piece of matching yarn to sew with. A piece too long will be difficult to work with.

Front side   Back side

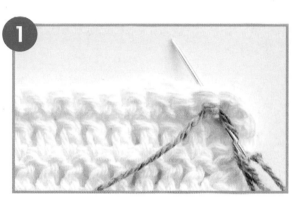

1 Using a threaded tapestry needle, secure the yarn close to the top right edge. Insert the needle from front to back through both pieces in the first stitch.

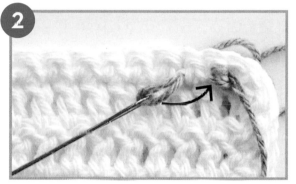

2 From back to front, bring the needle through the next stitch on the left. Draw the yarn through. From front to back, insert the needle into the first stitch and draw through.

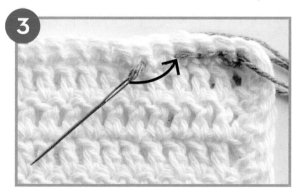

3 Skip the first stitch on the left. From back to front, bring the needle through the next stitch. Draw the yarn through. From front to back, insert the needle into the previous stitch and draw through.

4 Repeat step 3 across the seam. When complete, fasten off and weave in the yarn tails.

Tip: Match the size of your backstitches to the size of the crochet stitches in your piece.

Finishing Touch!

Chain Stitch Embroidery

Chain stitch embroidery is an easy way to add pops of color, free-form shapes, or lines on top of your crocheted piece.

- - - - - - - - - - - - - - - - -

Tip: Remember to yarn over on the opposite side.

- - - - - - - - - - - - - - - - -

1

Insert your hook from front to back into a stitch and yarn over on the back side. Draw the loop through to the front side in the space between 2 stitches. There is 1 loop on your hook.

2

Insert your hook from front to back into the next stitch and yarn over on the back side. Draw the loop through to the front side in the space between 2 stitches in the row above. There are 2 loops on your hook.

3

Draw the second loop through the first loop you made. There is now 1 loop on your hook.

4 Repeat steps 1–3 to continue the chain stitch embroidery.